P9-EDR-074

AFTER THE ARMIES
HAVE PASSED

for Julia,
and those who have helped

Contemporaries
Robert Hazel, Editor

AFTER THE ARMIES
HAVE PASSED

by
Jascha Kessler

New York University Press
New York   1970

Many of these poems have appeared in *The Saturday Review*, *Midstream*, *Trace*, *The Michigan Quarterly Review*, *Encounter*, *Kayak*, *Baroque* FTB, *The New York Times*, and *The Lace Curtain*.

CONTENTS

THE RETREAT

After the armies have passed
and we stand in the doorways
of our ruined, staring faces
wondering if we are safe,
the smell of pestilence comes
carried by our memories
stronger than words, and more true.

You have heard me without speech,
you have smiled, and consented
that we must leave ourselves here
burnt beyond recognition
as a gift to our old friends
who can remember nothing
but the quarrels and the tears.

Then we will force ourselves on
across the broken country
through the darkness of our thoughts:
it will be night, raining, cold,
two sick dogs will follow us
until we have disappeared
into our own silences.

THE MAD

1

No one expected children:
they had spoken in clear words
of grassy plains with low trees
rising, falling like the sea
below vague and paling skies—
not these hot damp jungle trails
choked by the flesh of children.

2

You're safe inside the movies
where everyone has his place
in the night among the stars
and voices and music play
what you want to know again
and you see yourself alive
doing what the others do.

3

The river was full of fish,
they said, but who could catch them?
It is like my memories,
I think, green, wild and shallow
through those harsh, broken passes,
and polluted by this town
to which it brought all my life.

4

On the beach, beneath the sun,
as though waiting for the tide
or the return of heaven,
stomachs, endless hordes of them—
nothing else but parasites,
sacks of meat with living mouths—
the beginning, and the end.

5

Forever and forever
these stone streets cross in my mind
like the place where I was born:
that quarter of the first town
preserved beneath the ruins
of your various new lives,
though no one knows it is there.

6

We'd come so far together,
struggling like two old convicts
sharing the risk of capture
and a minimum of food;
why did we quarrel right here,
just in sight of the border,
when neither could pass alone?

7

If after these corridors
and beyond those unlocked gates
there were beautiful persons
holding presents in their hands,
you might go on pretending
that you are talking to me
and that I want to listen.

THE HANDS

While I stood there in shame,
not sure if I should watch
or run to look for help
or run and save myself,
they fought over your hands
like drunk barbarians.

So good to me they'd been,
speaking with ten fingers
the language of the birds
that wake before morning,
as if they saw our thoughts
and flew from our mute hearts.

Now they are hard and cold,
broken off at the wrists,
senseless as the gestures
scattered through those lost rooms
these archaists restore—
who can conjure their warmth?

Or read their troubled lines?
Gone with all the rest, gone,
like the secret of your life
that came to me but once
with the body we shared
before we turned to stone.

Later, when I saw you,
you spoke to me, still kind,
as though nothing had happened
beside those buried years,
as though now you triumphed
in giving birth to me.
As though, as though, as though!

10

Let me say what is true:
once you held full hands out
in the terror of love,
and took them back, empty.
It happened long ago.

THE SELVES

Beneath those blank skies,
speechless, silent, stilled,
blind as stones frozen
under the snowfields,
forgotten by life,
everyone was dead.

In those winter woods
nothing but the wind
hard among the trees,
some small birds flitting
through their bleak branches
more like moths than birds.

Hoping for something
I stopped to listen:
a trunk swayed, creaked,
somewhere a twig cracked,
once a crow cried out,
a dog barked, far off.

They came at me then
along the snowpaths
pointing their fingers:
You! Liar! Coward!
Have you come here now
to carve your own name?

11

THE PRISONER

The doors had each been closed
when the sun smiled and struck;
but you remained outside
waiting for the robins,
as though they would fly back
to start your life once more.

All the others were here
come to hide from that light,
people who seemed like us:
they had stared at the stars
and sung back to silence,
vanished now, like the past.

But where had summer gone?
Far into the future,
like the love of hybrids
or strange simple fossils
rising in new mountains,
not yet a memory.

I called to you, I called
from behind my tired eyes,
because I was afraid
you would be lost out there,
wounded by the morning
and changed away from me.

How much I wanted you!
Now that we were all here
and locked in for the day,
we played in our torn beds,
pretending we were safe,
pretending we were young.

But you never answered,
and you never returned.
So that I taught myself
the things I thought I'd need:
I learned how to keep time,
I made an alphabet,
I showed the children death.

THE POETS

1

And when I rummaged in you
I found some bad romances,
their pages marked by a girl;
some stained teeth like buttons,
stale kisses older than love,
fake pearls, a bible, a muff.
None of it belonged to you.

2

But our secret's forgotten
when fanatic childhood goes,
just like the combination
of that favorite old lock.
When you asked me to find it
you meant to make me happy,
the old dog with his old trick.

3

A vacation wouldn't work—
best move on, just move away.
A walk through the museum,
though, to recall those old times,
preserved like premonitions
of our coming helplessness,
and then we would be ready.

4

One day he put on his best
and went out to see the town.
One day he threw a big party.
One day he ran round the house,
naked, roaring like a beast.
One day he played his records.
One day he wouldnt get up.

5

She wanted to very much.
Nothing fitted anything
although each had its own name
and belonged to her by right:
she nourished all her parts
as if she were a garden
that he would come to enjoy.

6

Still you couldn't understand.
There was blood on everything,
a network of molecules
enormous, invisible,
and neither dead nor alive.
It is the same everywhere.
We must bend our heads and drink.

7

It was an endless parade,
and they jammed Sixth Avenue:
Armies, Navies and Airplanes,
Clerks, Workers and Bosses,
Actors, Dancers, Deep Thinkers . . .
I knew you waited for me,
but I couldn't cross the street.

THE LOST

1

You raided our sepulchers,
for trinkets hacked up our graves
and ripped these numbed bones apart;
now we lie, restored, exposed,
scattered among broken tools
and blurred lines of joys we took,
but will never give to you.

2

That hair that held me to you,
thick as waterweeds, summer,
and smelling of moist, bright skin,
that hair you wore has vanished—
as though my life had been kept
in these crushed blue pigeon's eggs
thrown down from our tree today.

3

Out of my mouth those people
born like insects underground
swarmed up in black, humming clouds
and obscured the afternoon;
they were the barbarians
we had long been waiting for,
and we tore down these dead walls.

4

We can go where we damned please
as long as we look alive,
because the roads are open
right across the old mountains,
and because you remembered
a place that had sun and sky,
though you forget where it was.

5

I stood on a frozen street
right in the middle of town,
waiting with all the others
for a break in the weather
or a pretty girl to show.
When she came, weeping, naked,
no one would toss her his coat.

6

Suppose everything were glass,
the walls windows everywhere,
and through our transparent world
the fire of its core shone clear:
wouldn't you help me up then,
and wouldn't you understand
how much it hurts to love you?

7

There was no one in the room,
the mirror lied: lied lied lied!
Whenever she telephoned
she was frightened by his voice—
Do this that and the other—
as if there was time to think,
as though she were still alive.

THE MARRIAGE

You had hidden it from me
better than ever before.
I ransacked all your beauties
yet you made no resistance
to my terrible demands.
When I had finished, you said
"The place is inside the sun."

And then we fell fast asleep.
You dreamed that others would come,
bringing flowers and creamed cakes
like kind foreign gentlemen,
while I made good my escape
from that house of correction.
When we woke it was snowing.

Years later you dug me up:
rough bronze was what I'd become,
corroded by my own thoughts.
Yet neither could remember
what my purpose must have been
or how the way had been lost,
though we were just at our spring.

Oh we laughed when I came home
blackened and clawed by the sun
and that proud of my fat catch!
There was too much for us,
so you called our close friends in
to feast them on our blessings.
That night my fear filled the house.

And on the way from summer,
climbing through the mountains
up that unfamiliar road,
we slowed for breath near the top:
to the East lay our old seas
like the memories of birth,
like the shore we'd abandoned.

I was not one to sorrow
because I had died so soon—
you could eat our fruit alone.
So that autumn's come, and cold,
and you walk through maple groves
hearing only your footsteps
crush these bloody, brittle leaves.

You'd nowhere else to hide it:
I had crossed your continent
and swum out from your last rocks,
dazzled by that blind daylight
where you stand with open hands
like a loving wife, and say
"The place is inside the sun."

THE CONFUSIONS

1

A chest of old remedies
dried up and dusty with age
was all that remained to us
of our dozen long winters.
When that spring sickness returned
we were not prepared for life.
That was why we quarreled so.

2

How many fixed, faceless eyes
have you glanced into, curious,
in that fearful cut instant
of passage on the curved roads?
Invented by their own thoughts,
human more or less human,
these, the beings of the road.

3

Had I ever won gambles
I might have stopped this cheating.
My children are taught the law:
they gaze at me with calm eyes,
their faces clear as flowers,
empty of hope, or pity,
empty of comprehension.

4

Mouth to mouth, in our bodies
we found this ancient district
dying in our lost city
where we wait for each other
watching the late traffic run
recklessly with gouging lights
through cold stone streets past locked doors.

5

I wanted to find that book.
You never heard of that book?
He could not finish that book.
She wished she had read that book.
Had they always known that book?
We will need to have that book.
Was it after all that book?

6

In the darkness of your room
the smell of fish, weedy brine
and rotting mussels grows harsh—
as though the sea had rolled up
pouring in over my life,
and ebbed, and left these ruins,
when the moon dropped from the sky.

7

Everything held the secret
and everyone talked at once,
openly, simply, with smiles
that seemed to welcome one in—
as if we could understand,
as if we had always known
what was to be done with us.

THE CANNIBALS

And when the box was opened
it was a wedding present
brought by barbarous uncles—
don't you remember the words,
that old music, the dancing,
cakes and wine and so much food—
and how everyone kissed us?

And afterwards, when they left,
when we were alone at last,
poking through those gay ruins,
late towards our first morning,
when we were too tired to laugh,
we found it in a corner,
trembling in terrible fright?

And how we waited awhile
wondering what it could mean,
until the sun filled the room,
giving us no other choice—
don't you remember it now?
how we threw ourselves down then,
and how we killed it, and ate?

ONE SUNDAY AFTERNOON

Outside, the great gray boles
of the silent elm trees,
the suffering elm trees,
swayed in the storm's first winds.

Then massed low winter clouds
heaved and shifted and rolled
relentless over us
out of those torn black hills.

Inside, in our bedroom,
surrounded by roses
fading on the five walls,
we lay and watched it come.

We had no strength to move
together or apart,
but lay there cold, frightened,
waiting for each other.

Nothing we knew of life,
after ten years nothing,
but that the works of love
had passed with their seasons.

Then in that room's quiet,
as that house groaned and cracked,
there were words, whispered words
seeping like dust from those walls.

Dry spinsterish voices
insisted, insisted
we must quit, we must die:
there was no more to hope.

We listened, we listened
for hours to that sadness,
holding each other tight—
tight, tight. Until we wept.

TORTOISES

They all wandered in vague circles,
eating what they found or might catch,
sleeping where they dropped, night or day.
They survived, and told themselves tales:
We want nothing but this desert,
we are safe here, watched by angels,
and fitted for the lives we lead—
these beaks, these strong legs for our shells.

Centuries and centuries off,
as though it were there, virtual,
over this plunging, dim canyon,
across that flat waste of mesquite,
beyond that ridge of stone-dry hills,
like a spring of cold, fresh water,
is the place I have headed for,
each day one step, one step each night.

THE GIRL ON THE BILLBOARD

Your highways are open
and littered with bones,
but beyond the barbed wires
as far as they can see
your gentle land rolls brown
and waist-deep in summer.

They're crossing the high plains
at eighty miles an hour;
the noise of the radio,
the noise of the motor,
the noise of the parched wind,
batters them hard, like lust.

You have never seen them.
Or if you have, you think:
I'm sick of those drivers
all alike in their cars,
covered with sour dust,
hands trembling from the wheel,

thin long legs cramped like crows'
and pants creased at the crotch,
voices cracked with misuse
and thirst and loneliness—
behind those sunglasses
burnt eyes burning at me.

And you think: They stop here
because I'm beautiful,
because I might want them.
They know you're not, you don't.
Supposing they were free?
There's nowhere else to go.

THE ACCUSATION

There it was in your room,
dead, still warm but yes dead,
and you were the killer,
and no one else had come,
and no one had seen it
or heard that loud struggling.

What to do? It was late,
but never late enough.
You had friends, yet were they?
People seem skeptical
of someone else's luck;
police of course are worse.

Every old story
of every such room
came back to fill that night,
until you thought you'd wake
insane with hopeless fear
and never get out free.

There was one solution,
though, there was one for you—
tools lay in the drawers
and dishes on the shelves:
you cut, you trimmed, you cooked.
You sat. You ate yourself.

GAMBLERS ANONYMOUS

Oh let not the Lord be angry, and I will speak but this once;
Peradventure ten shall be found there. And he said, I will not
destroy it for ten's sake.   Genesis 18:32

He was very busy, he said,
he had to finish a big job
he took on a long time ago,
something to do with his uncle
the Button King of Babylon:
the old man had made a shrewd fortune,
but as for handing it around—
he was tight as an old maid's cunt.

So that was that, and there I was
out in the cold as usual
asking myself if I was nuts;
but it was good, and I knew it,
this time I knew it like I knew
the next one turning that corner
was a nigger without a coat,
red eyes burning me through the snow.

It wasnt even even dough;
I could have gotten ten to one,
look—ten to one on a sure thing!
Let the folks have first crack at it,
I thought; it's absolutely safe
and all they're risking is the nut—
like ten to one on this dollar
next chick round is hustling supper.

Just because they own the whole town
they think they're like god or something.
It's ten to one in your favor,
and you dont have to do a thing,
I told them, but believe in me
that *this* time it wasnt a hunch.
So? So I asked the old woman
to turn a trick once more. She did.

28

THE SOUVENIRS

for Lionel Trilling

1

Across the room, that woman
watched him with her hard brown eyes,
eyes bulging through their own strain
as he talked of those great eyes
that had vanished from our books.
"One would say we'd lost our souls."
Soft, gray, luminous, his eyes.

2

Once, and only once, I gazed
into eyes I'd never seen.
Though they showed no friendliness
they held no senseless hatred.
Wise they seemed, more than patient.
Yet when I smiled they mocked me
in return. Those eyes were mine.

3

When, over a filing case,
your hands paused and turned their palms
to reveal the strange pattern
in their lines, like the numbers
of one of those who lived on
after their own extinction,
I dared look up at your eyes.

4

In the streets I hunted their eyes
like an addict seeking friends
or a sad cruising fairy.
Towards evening, perhaps,
the fever would burn me out
and I might go home and eat,
as if I too were human.

5

Lambs, rabbits, calves, scalded swine,
turkeys, geese, fish and lobsters—
all the market's opened eyes,
edible and as blind as ours.
Admiring, we wandered through,
choosing among slaughtered friends
heads we hungered to devour.

6

That blind girl wished she could see
what we looked like in our flesh.
To us she was beautiful
and could not know what we knew:
that we looked at her with joy
but never at each other,
for we feared to see ourselves.

7

Your mouth waited for my kiss,
your eyes opened like morning
and I came to you gladly.
Inside your eyes it was night,
empty, illimitable,
through which I fell, forever,
towards remote, beating stars.

AFTER THE PARTY

Under the ceiling the smoke
wallowed yet, stained, used-up smoke;
the fire dropped into cinders,
throwing cracked gleams against them
where they sprawled, stale and stupid
in the trash of broken lives
they would never need again.

I climbed over their bodies
up the steep and littered stairs
turning only once to look
at what we had been doing
during that long evening,
as though I would forget it
in a lifetime of evenings.

Shining on the crusted snow
the light of a cold, late moon
spilled the silent rooms with ice;
somewhere a branch scraped the wall;
somewhere a tap was dripping;
and somewhere a girl sobbed
softly and beyond control.

Down that strict bleak hall I went,
past exhausted bedrooms
towards the malicious door
that had resisted my strength
till now—when it was so late—
when it swung in like a trap
upon your naked laughter.

LITTLE IVY LEAGUE

The icicles were dripping
and the cold gray clouds hung low;
the taps were in the maples,
the snowfields heavy, sunken.
White houses stained by winter
waited for the thaw to end,
and everyone had the flu.

If they werent stupid drunk.
There was enough to go round,
yes, of everything but good words,
laughter, and a friendly touch.
And what did we talk about
in those Adirondack days?
We were afraid of the Jews.

Our young physicist sang hymns
what Sundays he didn't ski.
All I knew of my best friend
was: he hit what he aimed at
and shot at everything,
his wife went to bed at eight
believing she was a witch.

How much warm milk with honey
do you think you can swallow?
Those winters are very long.
At the end we hunted ghosts
with music and candlelight:
Huron, Mohawk, Iroquois—
not one of them came to help.

I think something had gone wrong.
When the wet spring was rained out
those hot summer storms began:
people with incomes drove off
as those old shanties choked up
with black Southern families
trucked north to stoop for our beans.

It was a poor land round there,
living from the catalogue;
we found nothing to bid for
at their Saturday auctions
but ourselves, and we were poor.
Still if we'd offered these souls
would they know what they were for?

Some had babies, some tumors;
it was a lively piece of news
when Margaret's dinner burned;
a life of old storm windows
to be put up, taken down.
Those who survived would live on,
past eighty. The rest were dead.

AN ARTIST

for Fred Wight

"In my old age I have grown
abundant and determined,"
William Butler Yeats declared,
failed painter turned poet.
While I, writing thirty years,
consign my fictions to hell,
for they were but fictions all.

My eyes belong to my head,
and my head is full of eyes:
ten thousand words wouldnt do
to make an image, not one,
that should be as clear—clearer—
as the things I think they see
waiting patiently in me.

There is space, and there is fire;
there are bodies everywhere:
some are worlds, some barren stones,
some, like women stripped, bodies
nacreous or rose or masked,
lie hiding in their own forms
waiting patiently for me.

One year I pierced my canvas
with flame to get past those shams
of painted cloth; the next year
drilled through the wood I worked on,
painting breasts like eyes or stars
places I wanted to reach,
waiting patiently for me.

Nothing satisfies for long:
the brush the hand, or the forms
they throw out and leave behind
as though they shaped in my mind
merely to make me lose heart
because I see too much in here
waiting patiently for me.

But I know just what I want—
as if it were there for me,
there between my brush's tip
and the blank bright canvas wall:
it is a thing visible,
substanceless yet more than real,
waiting patiently for me.

Waiting patiently for me
at that hour when I wake
undressed by sleep, such small sleep,
a few moments out of life
in the arms of the one wife
I have always known as you,
you wait patiently for me.

THE CHILDREN

1

I had failed all of their tests
but you still believed in me
as if they didn't matter,
as though you were my real friend.
Get out, get away from me,
take the sun with you, and leave:
you don't need me anymore.

2

She was singing to herself
from the night that she was born,
and listening to her song
we could hear, or thought we heard,
There's an angel in a star,
and he burns my life away—
yet where are they, where are they?

3

They chose and chose and chose and
still I wasn't chosen in.
It was my bad luck, they laughed;
and when I dared to complain
they threw stones and knocked me down.
"Only fools cry," Father said,
"Look, your name is on that stone."

4

Our war began in springtime.
That summer we planned our fort,
collecting stuff to build it
and storing up the weapons.
When fall came round we waited,
watching the four streets all day.
Winter buried us with snow.

5

While my legs were in the cast
I had only this window.
Before the sun set she came
by herself and played that game.
I held my breath. Long long long.
Later I ran and told her.
Is that why she hates me so?

6

Always he'd love me, always.
And he showed me his closet,
which was like death, and naked.
But he knew where the fish were,
there, hidden in the deep pool,
after the woods, by the glade.
Yet I liked the quiet one.

7

Come here, they said, and do this.
Sit there, they said, and eat that.
Get up, lie down, go to sleep.
They said they said and they said.
There was just one place to hide
when all the others had been found:
here, where no one can see us.

THE HISTORY

1

It was a voice at morning
and again at the sunset:
words singing themselves, strange words,
old words, older than the world,
words not in any language,
though sometimes they seemed out there,
sometimes in here, in ourselves.

2

When I woke up, my father
stood there in the moon's shadow,
and I smelled the blood on him.
We were to run together
all night to the place prepared
long ago by the old ones.
There I would become a man.

3

So many came into me,
thrusting, heavy, whispering,
none the same yet all the same,
as though I was what they wished.
At noon, in the sun, I laughed,
and they turned away with shame.
What did they know, those children!

4

Once it had been so simple:
we walked in a great circle,
thrice round, and we understood.
When that circle was broken
and nothing could hold us back,
it all changed: now there were stars:
stars behind stars behind stars.

5

And the tribes fought each other,
the beasts, the birds, the fish, trees,
insects, the worms in the earth,
all intent upon their lives
in mutual, silent war,
as though the world would be theirs—
yet the mountain only slept.

6

I did not see what it meant
when you showed me house and field,
man and woman, and asked me
with your good smile to come in.
There was much work to be done,
the work of ten thousand years,
done, undone, before the end.

7

Our home crumbled at a touch,
like an apple made of dust.
We drifted away, apart,
out into the night of cold:
bits, fragments, brittle crystals
in which our selves had been sealed,
nameless now, and beyond death.

THE DEAD

The mines had been sealed off,
the cities forbidden;
winds stripped away the soil
and filled the rivers in;
but the killing went on
as though they wished to die.

The roads were blocked with cars
in which sat stubborn men
cradling guns in their laps,
and women whose faces
would never smile again,
long, dry, childless faces.

They sat inside themselves
waiting like emigrants
for permission to move—
until the crisis passed,
the last of their crises
in what seemed a lifetime.

And when they looked outside
toward the horizons,
the valleys and the hills
stretched crude and motionless
beneath a small, gray sun
silent as a stone bell.

Since the first announcement
they had been wandering
in these dim processions
across the vacant land:
there was nowhere to halt,
only the way ahead.

If they come at evening
out of the broken light,
or else before the dawn
when dew chills the dead earth,
they will ask a question
we answered long ago.

THE LOVER

Into your mouth my name
my head, my arms and all
my body following,
sinking into the night
that spreads its growing tide
over all the beaches.

Currents and dark channels
wandering like old roads
across a vague country;
silence, indifference,
a prison without walls
or other prisoners.

Naked I came, unarmed,
into your emptiness,
and stubbornly went on,
until my name, my thoughts,
and my swimming body
were all dissolved in you.

A STILL LIFE

There was a feeling, I know,
as if you had bought some fruit
and put it on the table
where we could watch it ripen:
apples, pears, and oranges,
figs and a few bananas—
the hearts of sweetness, and flies.

Suppose I had not come home,
suppose you'd forgotten me,
or grown tired of this page
as the light began to fade?
I see you closing windows,
or pausing at the mirror—
I see you touching your lips.

It is here, you whispered, here
and nowhere else that it was;
like the music of traffic
in our terrible city
it must be known to be heard—
and yet nothing is harder
than to listen to one's self.

There is the wine in the glass,
and the long evening drinks it;
there were words we waited for,
and they changed us like our lives;
but the night needs only night—
so that, being what we are,
we turn to our beginnings.

THE INHERITANCE

Of all the sisters he had
not one was fertile, not one.
They crowded about his days
imploring him for a word,
a touch, to keep them alive.
When he shut his mind up tight
they cursed him, and his children.

The woman was as swollen
with what I was to become
as a victim nine days drowned.
Yet it was not natural,
not pleasing, to discover
that the bottom of the sea
was the place where I must live.

After those ten million years
and a world of continents,
I was just as they had been,
like a fossil snail in coal:
the lines of a simple life
that had been lived without thought
yet would last longer than death.

Our wide August raft floated
down that long, slow Sunday path
among old ones and children,
and youths naked in their clothes.
Then you spoke one word, my name.
The leaves turned brown. It was winter.
It was now. I was alone.

You had expected kindness
from my memories, at least.
When you visited that park
in which you had found your love,
addicts of hunger and sadness
were drifting through the dim woods
like poor, lost, mangy mongrels.

But still, it was not something
dropped in one of those dark times,
like our old family ring
that had seemed precious as life
and which you lost yesterday—
it was still here, in ourselves,
and younger than our children.

So there was nothing left
of all we had been given;
and yet you woke today,
you sat up after a night
of tears of deathly struggle
against them and their angers,
and smiled at the new sunlight.

THE EXILES

for Claire Trotter

1

I thought I knew that language,
but could not read the pages
that glimmered before my eyes.
I was not drunk, not dreaming.
I was dazzled by these tears,
living tears wept long ago
and by other eyes than mine.

2

It seemed as though you knew me.
I was a street near your home.
Spring had come. You wore new shoes.
A ball bounced out from the curb
but you were scared by the cars.
Then summer, then winter came.
When spring returned, we had changed.

3

I had not slept or suffered;
yet, as the car climbed the hill
and you looked away, I knew—
long before we'd reached the top,
where we would halt, confounded
by that calm, shoreless desert—
that my mind had cracked like glass.

4

Her father owed her too much:
the kiss he never gave her
was bestowed by his brother,
in the fields, against her wish.
Twenty years it haunted her—
she did not know what she was
until they died, and told her.

5

I lay on my bed, waiting.
I had taken twenty years
from my life and made them one.
There was no more left for me.
Nothing could bring back my life.
No one but I knew the truth.
Soon it would come and kill me.

6

When I think of you, you come—
ten thousand miles are nothing.
Like the memory of love
your kind and naked body
stands here in silence, opened
to the dark jazz of this death.
If I knew your name, I'd speak.

7

Inside the stones there are birds,
and inside the birds, rivers;
in those rivers, little fish
and in those fish, the stars shine.
The stars were nothing but light.
Then they were dust. Then they fell.
How long ago that all was.

THE REVELATIONS

1

Now, when they are old and sick,
they say they have lied to us,
that we must learn the real use
of the only tools we have:
fingers and feet, and these jaws,
though later on sticks and stones
may prove to be good weapons.

2

Looking at you this morning
as you stared into the fumes
of your black and bitter cup,
I saw how far we had come:
between us there was nothing
but the past that we'd forgot,
that lay waiting for us now.

3

If I were the messenger
bringing fresh air from Delphi
like news of April flowers
after a lifetime of winters—
anemones and daisies,
such azures, scarlets and white
among those formless ruins . . .

4

When they left us behind here
they took just their lives with them,
which were all they could carry,
and but all that we wanted . . .
I meet them though, now and then,
in my dreams—these frightful dreams!
happy, doing what they like.

5

In the middle of the night
windows split, shattered and fell
as though invisible fists
went rapping them at random;
outside in that storm of glass
the streets were filled with black men,
mute, and patient, and unmoved.

6

Towards morning, blood rising
in the unlit antique squares
where those white fountains yet splashed
their pure and selfless music,
a dead stillness woke us up:
perhaps an hour remained,
perhaps not. We would make love.

7

If you walked out now, at noon,
to look across the desert
where colored broken mountains
crumble into boiling sands,
you would see that we're falling,
falling, falling at the sun,
and you would never come home.

THE RAFT

for Bill and Shirley Brice

I remember a city
maddened by its own people,
black, loud, shaken by machines,
where light burned the open eye
and air filled the lungs with pain;
there, whatever was, was right,
and no one looked at the sky.

And I remember those roads,
swift and merciless as lust,
that coiled about our city
like a living, shrinking mesh:
they were their own laws, the roads,
and their desires were obeyed,
gladly, as if we loved them.

And I remember silence,
as though everyone stopped
at midday just where he stood;
there were no clouds above us,
but high, high, blown by great winds,
silver specks sparkling
like motes in our swollen eyes.

And I remember thinking,
slowly, with dead clarity,
how I hated old people
for their money and their lies,
and pitied these clever youths
who swallowed all or nothing—
that I wished my friends near me.

Silent, we searched across time
through telescopes, wondering:
What books had he saved to read?
How would she have her baby?
Would it rain for you that year?
Had those natives slaughtered them?
I must invent a science.

Half-alive, this drifting world
exposed to the last forces
and far from the granite caves
in which are heaped years on years
the bones of our lost parents:
here men lay dreaming of women,
and the women dreamed of men.

And then the attack came down,
logically, by itself,
as it once did in that tale
when the waters rose and struck
and we found out we had lived
on a vanishing island . . .
Smiling, they said, "Now begin."

THE LOSERS

1

That first time you were naked
I cherished my dreams of you:
there was no one there at all.
The next you were in the flesh,
waiting to be found, like love.
The last time, you almost spoke.
I remember your long arms.

2

His anger moved in her mouth
like a prisoner's prayer:
the happiness they wanted
belonged to other people
who are cleverer than they
and live next door like neighbors,
yet much too far for comfort.

3

Ten years that struggle went on,
as if with these two bare hands
I took by the throat my mind
and fought it down in the dark,
panting, sweating, murmuring
like naked famished lovers
who would die if torn apart.

4

I was to call him master
though he was my hundredth man.
Pale, thin, cruel, wet, nervous—master!
And I to be his creature,
even my mind, like these breasts.
But what did he make of me?
Less than others had—and would.

51

5

Because I knew you loved me
I was no longer ashamed,
neither of my helplessness
nor of what I'd done to you:
it was your face I kneeled on,
it was your face that I crushed
six days, six nights, in that train.

6

Hair will grow into their eyes,
and sand will fill their nostrils;
their fingers will fuse like wood
and their feet freeze to black stones;
but they will be wide awake,
they will listen, they will think,
and they will want to make love.

7

Suddenly our road ended,
nowhere, in a waste of sage—
the last lights of America
had disappeared in the dark
a hundred miles behind us,
and out there, blocking the stars,
loomed vast old forms, the mountains.

REINCARNATION

How long had we been living
there in those slums of summer,
there in that dank, cursed ghetto
where flies fought over bad fruit
and the smoke of people's eyes
hung along the seething streets
through which we found no passage?

Nothing rare or good remained,
everything was second-hand,
used and reused like old books
whose words are strange or stupid:
although it was October
and they seemed sick of their past,
they would never let it go.

In our poor, bare, dusty room
we gnawed at one another,
rolling on the floor like dogs;
our windows, jammed half-open,
passed their angry shadows through
and filth that their hands flung up
fell in on us where we lay.

It was like a dream, we said,
and we were still like children;
there was no way out, we said,
or if there was, they knew us
by our walk, our low voices:
we were friendless, we were thieves,
and they hated us at sight.

When the rains began to fall
and the wind closed their shutters,
it was time for us to leave:
now that winter was coming
only the stones stayed behind,
the cold, black and ancient stones
glinting with indifference.

THE SLEEPER

My turn will come, you said,
and I shall wake you up
one summer afternoon
like rain in the window
you neglected to close,
and you will curse yourself.

Because your hand will hold
nothing but your own flesh,
dry as your opened mouth;
you will think of my name,
you will want to call me,
but your tongue will not move.

And in the other room
the radio's playing
that bad music—it blares
as though I were with you,
or you yourself were there—
yet you will be alone.

You will watch the warm rain
falling beyond the trees
on an empty meadow;
not a bird will fly past,
not a car will drive by,
and the day will not end.

It may be your own past,
an hour of memory
that has returned to you
or which you have become,
a time that may have been
part of you, or may not.

How you will want me then!
More than you want to live:
and you will discover
that every bit of me,
all that you thought you had,
is more than ever real.

HOMEKEEPING

I closed my eyes and walked
about the house where I
had lived for years, and sulked,
and ate my tongue, and cried.

I groped the hall for you,
my chair, the couch, our bed;
when I touched the window
how chilled I felt, afraid.

A dark mirror, so dark
to my ten famished fingers,
which closed, and would not work,
but gripped these angers.

Inside my mind your voice
sounded vague, vague to me;
old thoughts, old hopes, the curse
of love that's gone away.

"The best of our story
was that we'd never find
ourselves hurt, or sorry—
though broken by the wind."

"Shall we not meet again,
speak of our missing life,
asking when this began,
this death, this unbelief?"

How long you had waited,
I said to the dumb walls,
to see me so treated,
a prisoner, and fool!

SURFER IN WINTER

A half a glass of beer,
a plate of fish and chips,
a long cold foggy day:
out there on the water
slip slap slop like always
with a few gulls asleep.

They think it's monotonous,
they think it's just a fad
you will grow out of yet—
like you quit hide and seek,
driving the car too fast,
or touching every blouse.

But it's not that, not that;
there's a basic rhythm
that goes on forever,
and you sit out there and wait
and watch the steady swell
and take the one that counts.

Sometimes nothing happens.
Mostly nothing happens.
They break, you break, or both.
The day passes, a day
like all the other days:
the tide drops and you quit.

But sometimes there's a wave,
that certain lift you feel,
a shadow in the green,
and you know it's the one
and you're with it coming—
you're on, you're up, you're in.

There's never someone else.
There's only you alone.
If it's right and you're right,
you're walking on water,
coming in from the sea
as if you were just born—
though you never reach shore.

EMIGRANTS

They wanted our house,
our clothes, our money,
they seized everything,
everything we had—
then they took our skins.

All that year we walked
towards the border,
followed by their eyes,
as if they pitied
or could understand.

In time, somewhere else,
we grew whole again
and our lips made sounds
which, if not human,
are the words we have.

They cannot find us
or destroy us now,
they have forgotten
that we ever lived—
Here we wait for them.

THE RESURRECTION

For eyes I gave you rubies
twin emeralds for nostrils
I set your mouth with sapphires
and filled your ears with pearls
all the rest I made of gold
so that though my gifts were praised
when they brought you back to love
their hands should never stain you.

And then I forgot your name,
forgot where I laid you down
as the bells began to ring—
it was just noon I think—
our rotten priests were preaching:
We must fight! and We must pray!
but no one would, no one could,
and their troops went marching by.

We were given up as lost.
Long years, bad years fell on us:
coarse weeds grew in our dry laps
goats and sheep flocked against us
their foul swine rooted in us
mongrels came to scratch and shit—
yet we refused to stand up.
That brook saved us from the death.

After so many mornings
a last morning came to us:
the sun broke through our hard sleep
and tore away these covers.
Yet, despite your nakedness,
I could not apprehend you.
Later, in that library,
dim, cold people seized my arms.

And afterwards we wandered
with the roads, everywhere;
sleety clouds pressed on the hills
and closed against the city,
streets and houses turned to stone
and the people spat with hate
because we passed their doors by . . .
yet we'd been there, long ago.

And so it went, on and on,
through all those days of our lives
and in the dreams of our nights:
there was nothing we could make,
there was nothing we could do
but wait, and wish for an end.
When it came, we were surprised
to find ourselves waiting still.

Now I recall your story
as though it had been mine,
as though I woke at midnight
and lay for hours appalled
by its incessant vision
like those alien paintings
in the old museums groups
of tired tourists must endure.

Let me touch you now, hold you
let me find you warm and soft
let me take away the things
that are neither you nor yours
let me speak to you once more
looking into your kind eyes—
as if you would come to me
as if we lived here again.

THE DREAM

for Austin Warren

I had lost my cleverness
and my humor, I had lost
my strength, my love and my hate:
I could not find the true word
which I must say to find you—
and yet you were beside me,
to the left and just behind.

I changed again and again
but always seemed just the same;
I killed and cursed, wept and fought
my way to an unknown house
where I stopped, baffled, and heard
a greeting so familiar
that I knew it must be you.

And here was my professor
seated at his writing desk
in his starched white doctor suit;
the Midwest air, hot and wet,
filled his book-lined room with death,
and as he smiled, smiled at me,
I saw he was drunk, and mad.

He knew a secret doctrine
by which bourbon would unlock
the history of my face,
the mystery of my race,
if I'd wait with him for dawn:
when I stooped to shake him
he spoke his prayers—in Greek.

There was nothing more to do.
As I turned from him, he cried
"Watch me, and I'll show the way!"
He wore a long golden robe
and a shining golden crown:
as my torchlight struck his face
he leaped laughing from the room.

Our car crashed in a plowed field
and burnt itself to nothing;
we walked on across country
stumbling through the morning mist:
cows danced by with full udders,
and a stallion galloped mares
round us in thundering rings.

Pigeons sprang up at our feet,
and long files of geese flew past
on our right, to the Northwest,
the way that we were going:
and when we found the great trees
shading the slowing river
we took off our clothes, and slept.

THE DEPARTURE

I had known who you were
long before I woke up
and found you beside me,
before I turned the car,
left, down an unknown street
full of such poor people
who stared as we drove through.

At the end, at the wharf,
the ship was waiting still,
the great old famous Queen
with the thousand cabins
and the holds vast enough
for all that was needed
on the long excursion.

My mind was not made up.
And I had no money.
What had I left undone?
Yet I could not return.
But where were they going?
It had not been announced.
And I had not been asked.

While the gulls screamed and swooped
we crept on board her then
over an unwatched plank.
Behind us the city
that had been deserted
so many years ago
spread silent, empty, dead.